International Political Communication

Understanding the Issues

Written by:

Dr. David K. Ewen

ISBN: 9798321812488
Imprint: Independently published by Enterprise College

Cover art by Juliana Kozoski via Unsplash

Dr. David K. Ewen

About the Book

In his insightful book, Dr. David K. Ewen, who serves as an Ambassador Professor, delves into the complex world of international communication and its profound impact on global power dynamics. Dr. Ewen's work is a thorough exploration of how modern communication technologies have started to dissolve traditional boundaries, leading to significant shifts in the way power is distributed and exercised around the world. Through his comprehensive analysis, the author brings to light the evolving nature of international relations in the digital age, marked by an increasingly interconnected global landscape.

Dr. Ewen argues that the advent of the internet and social media has radically transformed the flow of information, making it more democratic and accessible to people across different continents. This democratization of information has, in turn, empowered individuals and non-state actors, enabling them to play a more significant role in the international arena. The book illustrates how these changes are challenging the conventional notions of sovereignty and control that nations have traditionally held, forcing a reevaluation of how power is understood and wielded on the global stage.

One of the key insights from Dr. Ewen's book is the concept of a "communication shift." This idea encapsulates the transition from a world where information dissemination was controlled by a few powerful entities to a more decentralized and participatory communication landscape. This shift has not only affected the dynamics of international politics but also has implications for diplomacy, governance, and social movements. The author meticulously examines how this shift is reshaping the strategies and policies of states and international organizations, as they seek to navigate the challenges and opportunities presented by this new era of global communication.

Furthermore, Dr. Ewen explores the potential of international communication to foster greater understanding and cooperation among nations. He posits that by eroding physical and metaphorical borders, global communication can pave the way for a more collaborative and inclusive international system. However, he also cautions against the risks associated with this transformation, including the spread of misinformation, cyber warfare, and the erosion of cultural identities.

About the Author

Dr. David K. Ewen embodies the spirit of innovation and dedication in the realms of education and international entrepreneurship. As the visionary founder of Enterprise College and Global Studies University, he has not only laid the groundwork for these institutions but also actively shapes their future as an Ambassador Professor. His role extends beyond administrative duties, diving deep into fostering an environment of learning and global awareness that is reflective of the interconnected world we live in today.

Since embarking on his entrepreneurial journey in 1994, Dr. Ewen has collaborated with diverse teams spanning continents—from the bustling cities of Asia and the cultural mosaics of the Middle East to the historical landscapes of Europe, the expansive terrains of Russia, and the vibrant cultures of South America. These experiences have not only enriched his understanding of global markets and cultures but have also infused his educational initiatives with a unique international perspective.

Dr. Ewen's academic journey is equally impressive, marked by significant achievements that have fortified his role as an educator and leader. Holding both a Master's in Education (M.Ed.) and a Doctorate in Education (Ed.D.), he possesses a deep understanding of educational theories and practices, which he adeptly applies to create learning environments that are both engaging and effective. These credentials are not just symbols of personal achievement but are foundational to his approach in merging theoretical knowledge with practical application, ensuring that students are prepared for the complexities of the globalized world.

What sets Dr. Ewen apart in his field is his ability to weave together his vast international experience with his robust academic background, creating educational models that are relevant, dynamic, and impactful. Through his work, he demonstrates the power of education to transcend traditional boundaries, fostering a generation of learners who are not only knowledgeable but also culturally astute and empathetic to global issues. His commitment to education and international collaboration serves as an inspiration to many, highlighting the potential for meaningful change when education and real-world experience converge.

Table of Contents

Chapter 1: International Communication

The advent of global communication has ushered in a new era for international relations, fundamentally altering the way nations interact, govern, and forge connections. This shift, primarily fueled by the erosion of traditional borders and the ascendancy of new media technologies, presents a labyrinth of both challenges and opportunities that are reshaping the international political landscape.

Traditionally, nation-states operated within well-defined territorial boundaries, with governments exercising sovereign control over the flow of information, cultural exchange, and diplomatic communications within their borders. However, the rapid proliferation of digital communication technologies has blurred these lines, enabling information, ideas, and cultural content to traverse the globe instantaneously. This has not only diminished the control states have over information but also challenged the notion of sovereignty itself, as the digital realm often operates beyond the reach of traditional governance structures.

The dual nature of global communication's impact is evident in its ability to both homogenize and diversify. On one hand, the global spread of pop culture, often criticized as "Coca-Colonization," suggests a trend toward cultural homogenization. On the other hand, the same digital platforms that facilitate this spread also empower previously marginalized voices, allowing them to assert their identity, share their perspectives, and challenge dominant narratives on the global stage. This dynamic has turned global communication channels into arenas where economic, political, and cultural boundaries are constantly being negotiated and contested.

Moreover, the rise of global communication has led to a significant shift in power dynamics within international relations. The immediate and borderless nature of digital communication has undermined traditional top-down approaches to governance and diplomacy, challenging established hierarchies and power structures. This democratization of communication has enabled a wider range of actors to participate in the international dialogue, from non-state entities and civil society organizations to individual activists and influencers.

This transformation is further complicated by the paradox of globalism and its discontents. While global communication fosters a sense of interconnectedness and shared global identity, it also exacerbates tensions related to nationalism, regionalism, localism, and fundamentalism. These tensions reflect the uneven levels of economic development and cultural integration across the globe, with modern communication technologies often amplifying these disparities rather than bridging them.

The shift from traditional "push" media, where content is delivered from a central source to a passive audience, to "pull" media, characterized by active audience engagement and content selection, represents another dimension of this transformation. This shift has rendered obsolete the conventional "North-South" or "developed-developing" models of international communication, paving the way for a more multi-faceted and egalitarian global public sphere.

As global communication continues to redefine the international political landscape, it poses significant implications for governance, diplomacy, and cultural exchange. The empowerment of new actors and the challenge to traditional authority structures underscore the need for adaptive governance models that can navigate the complexities of this new reality. The international community is thus faced with the task of harnessing the potential of global communication to foster greater understanding and cooperation, while addressing the challenges it presents to ensure a more inclusive and equitable global order.

Chapter 2: Eroding Borders

The transformative power of global communication technologies, notably the internet and social media, has had a profound impact on the traditional constructs that have long defined nation-states. These digital platforms have effectively diminished the physical and metaphorical boundaries that once demarcated sovereign territories, ushering in an era where information flows freely and boundlessly across the globe. This unprecedented access and exchange of information across borders represent a significant challenge to the sovereignty and control historically wielded by states, fundamentally altering the landscape of governance and diplomacy.

Traditionally, the sovereignty of a nation-state was closely tied to its ability to control the flow of information within its borders, a critical aspect of maintaining authority and governance. The state's role as the primary gatekeeper of information allowed for the regulation of media, the censorship of dissenting voices, and the shaping of national narrative and identity. However, the advent of global communication technologies has eroded this control, making it increasingly difficult for states to monitor and manage the information that enters and exits their borders.

Social media platforms, in particular, have democratized the production and dissemination of information, enabling individuals and non-state actors to broadcast their voices on the global stage. This has led to a more participatory form of communication, where traditional hierarchies of information flow are challenged, and power dynamics are shifted. Citizens now have the tools to organize, mobilize, and express dissent in ways that were previously unimaginable, often circumventing government controls and censorship.

The impact of this shift is multifaceted, affecting not only governance within states but also the dynamics of international relations. Diplomacy, once the purview of state actors and conducted through formal channels, now unfolds in real-time on digital platforms, where diplomatic statements and interactions are subject to public scrutiny and engagement. This has introduced a new level of transparency and immediacy to international relations, but also a potential for miscommunication and escalation.

Moreover, the ability of information to cross borders with ease has led to increased interconnectivity among nations, fostering a global consciousness and shared culture. However, it also raises concerns about the erosion of cultural identities, the spread of misinformation, and the potential for external interference in domestic affairs. The challenge for nation-states in this new era is to navigate the delicate balance between harnessing the benefits of global communication technologies for economic, social, and diplomatic purposes, while mitigating the risks to sovereignty, security, and cultural integrity.

In essence, global communication technologies have initiated a profound transformation in the way information is shared and consumed, challenging the traditional parameters of nation-state sovereignty and reshaping the landscape of global governance and diplomacy. This dynamic environment presents both opportunities and challenges, requiring a reevaluation of traditional governance models and diplomatic practices in the face of an increasingly interconnected and digital world.

Chapter 3: Dual Impacts

The phenomenon of global communication has ushered in an era of unprecedented connectivity, profoundly influencing cultures worldwide. This era has been characterized by the widespread dissemination of a uniform pop culture, a trend often criticized as "Coca-Colonization," where dominant cultural products and values, typically of Western origin, permeate global markets, potentially eroding local cultures and traditions. This critique highlights concerns over cultural homogenization, where diverse traditions and identities are overshadowed by a monolithic cultural narrative. However, this is only one facet of the impact of global communication.

Parallel to the spread of a homogenized culture, global communication platforms have also served as vital spaces for empowering marginalized voices, illustrating the complex dual nature of these technologies. Social media, blogs, and various other digital platforms have democratized content creation and distribution, allowing individuals and groups from diverse backgrounds to share their stories, perspectives, and cultural expressions with a global audience. This empowerment has provided a counterbalance to the forces of cultural homogenization, offering a stage for the rich tapestry of global diversity to be showcased and celebrated.

Moreover, these platforms have transformed into battlegrounds where economic, political, and cultural divides are openly contested. The internet has enabled activists, minority groups, and disenfranchised communities to organize, mobilize, and challenge existing power structures. Social media campaigns, online petitions, and viral videos have become powerful tools for advocacy and change, highlighting issues of social justice, human rights, and environmental concern. This dynamic underscores the transformative potential of global communication to not only bridge divides but also to amplify calls for change and accountability.

However, the same tools that empower can also divide. The global reach of communication technologies has sometimes intensified divisions, spreading misinformation, and fueling polarization. The ease with which content can be shared and the algorithms that govern visibility on these platforms often promote sensational and divisive content, exacerbating tensions. This highlights the paradoxical nature of global communication: its ability to both unify and divide.

Basically, the landscape of global communication is a complex and multifaceted one, where the forces of cultural homogenization coexist with the empowering potential of digital platforms. These platforms have emerged as critical arenas for the contestation of economic, political, and cultural divides, demonstrating the profound impact of communication in shaping the modern world. As we navigate this landscape, the challenge lies in leveraging these technologies to foster understanding, inclusivity, and positive social change, while being mindful of their potential to exacerbate divisions and undermine cultural diversity.

Chapter 4: Power Dynamics

The ascendancy of global communication technologies has ushered in a transformative era in world politics, significantly altering the established dynamics of power and influence. This transformation challenges the foundational theories of international relations that have long guided our understanding of global power structures. Historically, these structures were defined by hierarchical relationships between nation-states, with power often concentrated in the hands of a few dominant players on the global stage. However, the proliferation of digital communication platforms has disrupted these traditional hierarchies, catalyzing a shift towards a more decentralized and diffused landscape of power.

This shift is primarily driven by the democratizing effect of the internet and social media, which have empowered individuals and non-state actors to participate more actively in the global discourse. These platforms have provided a voice to those who were previously marginalized in international discussions, allowing them to exert influence and shape outcomes in ways that were once the exclusive domain of sovereign states and multinational corporations. Activists can mobilize global public opinion on issues ranging from climate change to human rights, small businesses can access global markets with ease, and individuals can engage in cross-border cultural exchanges, all contributing to a more interconnected and multipolar world.

The implications of this transformation are profound. Traditional metrics of power, such as military strength and economic might, while still significant, are increasingly being complemented by the ability to influence global narratives and shape public opinion. Soft power, the power of attraction and persuasion, has become more pivotal in the digital age, where ideas and ideologies can spread rapidly across borders. The success of a nation's foreign policy, therefore, may hinge not only on its diplomatic and economic leverage but also on its ability to effectively communicate and resonate with a global audience.

Moreover, the rise of global communication has introduced new challenges in the exercise of power on the international stage. The speed and scale at which information can be disseminated mean that states must navigate a more complex and fluid information environment. Misinformation and cyber warfare have emerged as potent tools that can be used to undermine political stability, influence elections, and sway public opinion, posing new threats to national and global security.

The changing landscape necessitates a reassessment of how power is defined and exercised in the realm of international relations. Traditional theories, which emphasized the role of states and formal institutions, must adapt to account for the influence of digital networks and the myriad actors they empower. This includes recognizing the significance of non-state actors, the impact of transnational networks, and the importance of information and communication technologies as tools of power and influence.

Chapter 5: Globalism's Paradox

The advent of global communication technologies has been a double-edged sword in the context of international relations and cultural exchange. On one hand, these technologies have played a pivotal role in supporting global integration, fostering a sense of interconnectedness among people across the world. They have facilitated the exchange of ideas, cultures, and information, contributing to a more unified global community. This phenomenon has been instrumental in promoting cooperation among nations, enhancing economic interdependence, and fostering mutual understanding among diverse cultures.

However, the same global communication networks that promote integration also serve as platforms for its opposition, notably nationalism, regionalism, and other identity-based movements. These technologies provide a means for communities and individuals to express and organize around their unique identities, often in response to the perceived threats of globalization. Social media, in particular, has become a powerful tool for mobilizing nationalist and regionalist sentiments, allowing groups to amplify their voices and advocate for their interests on the global stage.

This paradoxical nature of global communication technologies reflects the underlying disparities in economic development and cultural integration across the world. While globalization has brought about unprecedented levels of wealth and cultural exchange, its benefits have not been evenly distributed. Many communities perceive globalization as a force that undermines their economic prospects and dilutes their cultural heritage. In this context, global communication technologies can serve as a rallying point for those seeking to resist the homogenizing effects of globalization, providing a space for the articulation of alternative visions of society based on local or national identities.

Moreover, the capacity of these technologies to both connect and separate underscores the complex dynamics of contemporary globalization. They have the power to bring people together, facilitating dialogue and understanding across cultural divides. Yet, they also have the capacity to deepen divisions, allowing for the rapid spread of misinformation and the reinforcement of echo chambers where like-minded individuals reinforce each other's beliefs without exposure to differing viewpoints.

Generally speaking, global communication technologies embody the contradictions of globalization itself. They are at once vehicles of integration, breaking down barriers between nations and cultures, and tools of division, enabling the proliferation of movements that seek to assert distinct identities in the face of globalizing forces. This dual role highlights the nuanced impact of modern technologies on the global landscape, demonstrating their ability to both bridge and widen the gaps between different parts of the world. As such, navigating the challenges and opportunities presented by global communication requires a careful balance, recognizing the potential of these technologies to foster a more integrated world while also acknowledging their role in promoting diversity and difference.

Chapter 6: Communication Shift

The evolution from traditional "push" communication methods, where content is delivered from a central source to a passive audience, to "pull" technologies exemplified by the internet, marks a significant transformation in the landscape of information exchange. This transition has revolutionized the way information is shared and consumed, shifting the power dynamics of communication from the hands of a few broadcasters to the fingertips of the global population. In the era of push communication, media outlets, governments, and corporations had the primary control over the flow of information, deciding what news, entertainment, and cultural content would reach audiences. This model reinforced a top-down approach to knowledge dissemination, often reflecting the interests and perspectives of those in power.

The advent of the internet and other digital platforms, however, has ushered in the age of pull communication, where individuals actively seek out and select the information that interests them. This model democratizes access to information, enabling users to bypass traditional gatekeepers and explore a diverse array of sources. Social media platforms, blogs, forums, and online publications offer alternative narratives and perspectives, contributing to a more pluralistic information environment. The user's ability to interact with, comment on, and share content further amplifies this effect, encouraging participatory culture and community engagement.

This paradigm shift has profound implications for the "North-South" models of communication, which historically depicted a flow of information from developed, "Northern" countries to developing, "Southern" ones. These models were criticized for perpetuating imbalances in information exchange and cultural dominance, with the Global North setting the agenda and framing the narratives that shaped global perceptions. The internet, by facilitating access to a multitude of voices and perspectives, has challenged this unidirectional flow of information. It has enabled individuals and organizations in the Global South to share their stories directly with a global audience, fostering a more balanced and reciprocal exchange of information.

The result is a more egalitarian global dialogue, where the distinctions between who produces information and who consumes it are increasingly blurred. Individuals from different parts of the world can engage in direct conversation, share experiences, and collaborate on equal footing. This has the potential to bridge cultural divides, promote mutual understanding, and challenge stereotypes and prejudices perpetuated by one-sided narratives.

However, while the internet and digital technologies have the potential to democratize communication and foster a more egalitarian dialogue, challenges such as digital divides, censorship, and misinformation remain. Access to technology is not uniform, and disparities in digital literacy and infrastructure can limit participation in the global conversation. Moreover, the vast amounts of information available online require critical evaluation skills to navigate effectively.

Overall, the transition from push to pull communication technologies has transformed the global information landscape, challenging traditional models of communication and fostering a more inclusive and participatory global dialogue. This shift represents a significant step toward democratizing information exchange, but it also highlights the ongoing need to address the challenges that accompany our increasingly connected world.

Chapter 7: New Actors

The digital age has profoundly reshaped the international political and social landscape, particularly in how global challenges are addressed and the actors involved in these processes. One of the most significant shifts has been the elevation of non-state actors, such as NGOs, civil society organizations, multinational corporations, and even influential individuals, who now play pivotal roles in international affairs. Enabled by digital technologies, these actors can mobilize resources, influence public opinion, and enact change at a speed and scale previously unattainable, challenging the traditional state-centric model of international relations.

Simultaneously, the importance of international institutions in mediating global challenges has become more pronounced. Organizations such as the United Nations, the World Health

Organization, and the International Monetary Fund are expected to coordinate responses to transnational issues like climate change, pandemics, and economic crises, which are beyond the capacity of any single nation to resolve. The interconnectedness facilitated by digital communication means that the actions or policies of these institutions have a more immediate and direct impact on the global populace, underscoring their significance in the international order.

However, the effectiveness of these international institutions in navigating the complexities of the digital age has come under scrutiny. Criticisms often center on issues of representation and equity, with many arguing that these bodies reflect the interests of a select group of nations or are too removed from the realities of the people they aim to serve. The decision-making processes within these institutions are sometimes seen as opaque or undemocratic, leading to calls for comprehensive reform. The challenge lies in adapting these institutions to a world where information flows freely and power is more dispersed, necessitating a more inclusive and participatory approach to global governance.

The rise of non-state actors further complicates this dynamic, as it challenges the traditional sovereignty of states and the authority of international institutions. While these actors can complement the efforts of states and institutions, their diverse agendas and methods of operation also introduce new variables into international diplomacy and governance. For instance, the ability of a multinational corporation to impact economic policy or an NGO to shape environmental agendas highlights the complex interplay between state and non-state actors in the digital age.

The need for democratic reform and equitable governance in international institutions is not just about improving efficiency or transparency; it's about reimagining global governance in a way that reflects the realities of the 21st century. This includes acknowledging the role of digital technologies in empowering a broader range of actors, ensuring that governance structures are responsive to the needs and voices of a diverse global populace, and fostering collaboration across borders and sectors. The goal is to create a more democratic, equitable, and effective system of global governance that can address the pressing challenges of our time, leveraging the strengths of both state and non-state actors while mitigating the risks associated with their increased influence.

Pulling all this together tells us that the digital age demands a reevaluation of how global challenges are addressed and by whom. The elevation of non-state actors and the critical role of international institutions in this new landscape highlight the need for reforms that ensure these entities can effectively navigate the complexities of global governance while remaining accountable to the communities they serve.

Chapter 8: Conclusion

The transformative impact of global communication on international relations is a defining feature of the contemporary global landscape. As digital technologies continue to evolve at a breakneck pace, they are erasing old boundaries and forging new connections, fundamentally altering the way nations interact, collaborate, and compete on the world stage. This digital revolution presents a dual-edged sword: on one side, it offers unprecedented opportunities for collaboration, allowing for more efficient and effective coordination on a range of global issues. On the other, it challenges traditional power structures, forcing a reevaluation of long-standing diplomatic practices and norms.

The ability of global communication to bring together diverse actors from across the world has facilitated new forms of cooperation that were previously unimaginable. International organizations, governments, civil society, and individuals can now share information, resources, and strategies in real-time, enhancing their ability to respond to crises, coordinate policy responses, and mobilize support for global initiatives. This has been particularly evident in responses to global challenges such as climate change, public health emergencies, and humanitarian crises, where the rapid exchange of information and collaborative platforms have been crucial to the international community's ability to act.

However, the same technologies that enable these collaborations also pose significant challenges to traditional power dynamics. The democratization of information has empowered non-state actors and individuals, giving them the tools to influence public opinion, mobilize resources, and even shape policy outcomes. This shift challenges the monopoly on information and narrative control that states, and established institutions once held, introducing a more decentralized and pluralistic international order. Moreover, the rapid spread of information can also exacerbate tensions, spread disinformation, and destabilize traditional alliances, adding layers of complexity to international diplomacy.

The erosion of traditional boundaries by global communication technologies is not limited to the digital realm; it also has tangible effects on political, economic, and social landscapes. The global flow of information has facilitated economic integration, cultural exchange, and social connectivity, but it has also raised concerns about sovereignty, cultural homogenization, and the digital divide. As information transcends borders, nations grapple with the implications for national security, cultural preservation, and economic inequality, highlighting the need for new frameworks to govern the flow of digital information and its impact on global relations.

In this context, the international community stands at a crossroads. To harness the potential of global communication for positive outcomes, there must be a concerted effort to adapt to this new reality. This requires not only technological innovation but also diplomatic agility, cultural sensitivity, and a commitment to equitable development. Policymakers, diplomats, and leaders must engage in open dialogue, forge new partnerships, and develop international norms that reflect the interconnected nature of the world today. This includes addressing the digital divide to ensure that all nations have the opportunity to participate in the digital revolution, protecting the integrity of information to combat misinformation and cyber threats, and promoting cultural exchange to foster mutual understanding and respect.

Ultimately, the role of global communication in shaping the future of international relations is undeniable. As it continues to redefine the contours of the global community, the challenge lies in steering this digital revolution toward outcomes that enhance cooperation, promote peace, and ensure prosperity for all. The path forward is complex, requiring a delicate balance between embracing the opportunities presented by digital technologies and mitigating their risks. Yet, with thoughtful leadership and collective action, the international community can navigate this digital landscape to build a more connected, resilient, and equitable world.

Dr. David K. Ewen